CHAIN REACTIONS

From Greek Atoms to Quarks

Discovering Atoms

Sally Morgan

Heinemann
LIBRARY

www.heinemann.co.uk/library

Visit our website to find out more information about Heinemann Library books.

To order:

☎ Phone 44 (0) 1865 888066

📄 Send a fax to 44 (0) 1865 314091

💻 Visit the Heinemann Bookshop at www.heinemann.co.uk/library to browse our catalogue and order online.

Produced for Heinemann Library by White-Thomson Publishing Ltd, Bridgewater Business Centre, 210 High Street, Lewes, East Sussex BN7 2NH

First published in Great Britain by Heinemann Library, Jordan Hill, Oxford OX2 8EJ, part of Harcourt Education.

Heinemann Library is a registered trademark of Harcourt Education Ltd.

Consultant: Ann Fullick
Commissioning Editors: Andrew Farrow and
    Steve White-Thomson
Editor: Sonya Newland
Proofreader: Catherine Clarke
Design: Tim Mayer
Picture Research: Amy Sparks
Artwork: William Donohoe

Originated by RMW
Printed and bound in China by Leo Paper Group Ltd

10 digit ISBN 043118657X
13 digit ISBN 978-0-431-18657-3
11 10 09 08 07
10 9 8 7 6 5 4 3 2 1

British Library Cataloguing in Publication Data
Morgan, Sally
From Gas Clouds to Particle Accelerators: Discovering Atoms
539.7

A full catalogue record for this book is available from the British Library.

Acknowledgements
The author and publisher would like to thank the following for allowing their pictures to be reproduced in this publication: Corbis pp. 5 (Pierre Vauthey/Corbis Sygma), 6 (Archivo Iconografico, S.A.), 8 (Bettmann), 9 (Massimo Listri), 18 (Stefano Bianchetti), 21 (Bettmann), 22 (Bettman), 27 (Lester V. Bergman), 29 (DK Limited), 34 (Krause, Johansen/Archivo Iconografico, SA), 49 (Hulton-Deutsch Collection), 55 (Roger Ressmeyer); iStockphoto.com pp. 7 (Maartje van Caspel), 25 (Stephan Hoerold), 26 (George Toubalis), 36 (Jackie DesJarlais), 45 (George Argyrolpoulos), 47 (Dane Wirtzfeld), 54 (Maciej Noskowski); NASA pp. 41, 43; Science Photo Library pp. 4 (Philippe Plailly), 11 (Andrew Lambert Photography), 13 (Andrew Lambert Photography), 16, 20, 23 (Charles D. Winters), 35 (Ted Kinsman), 40 (American Institute of Physics), 48 (Patrice Loiez), 50 (ArSciMed), 52 (Philippe Plailly/Eurelios), 53 (Julian Baum); Topfoto.co.uk pp. 10, 12 (HIP), 14 (HIP), 15, 17 (HIP), 24 (HIP), 28, 30, 32 (Roger-Viollet), 37 (HIP), 46 (Photri).

Cover image courtesy of Science Photo Library (Mehau Kulyk).

Cover design by Tim Mayer.

Contents

Any words appearing in the text in bold, **like this**, are explained in the Glossary.

Discovering atoms

Imagine hurtling across the galaxy at speeds approaching the speed of light, visiting new planets, and even discovering life elsewhere in the Universe. You probably think that's just science fiction. But in 50 or 60 years' time it is possible that scientists will have learnt how to harness the energy locked up in atoms and use it to power spacecraft.

Atoms are the basic building blocks of all the **matter** that makes up everyday objects. A desk, a chair, the air – even you – are made up of atoms. There are 90 types of atom that occur naturally, and another 25 that scientists have made artificially in laboratories.

The story of the atom

The story of the atom starts about 400 BC, when Greek **philosophers** were discussing what matter was made of. A man named Democritus came up with the idea that if something could be cut into the smallest piece possible, it would still be the same object, with the same properties. Democritus was also the first person to use the word "atom".

This image shows gold atoms on a substance called graphite. The gold atoms are yellow, red, and brown. The graphite atoms are green. Pictures of atoms like this are taken using a special machine called a scanning tunnelling microscope.

Much of today's research into atoms is carried out in specially built facilities, such as this one at the Centre for European Nuclear Research (CERN) in Switzerland.

Democritus' idea became known as the atomistic theory. However, another philosopher – Aristotle – came up with his own theory, and this was the one that people believed for nearly 2,000 years. Eventually scientists were able to prove that Aristotle was wrong and Democritus was right.

In this book you will find out how scientists unravelled the secrets of the atom. It was not an easy journey. In some countries, the belief that Aristotle was correct was so strong that it was against the law to even suggest that the atomists might be right. In addition to this, atoms are far too tiny to be seen by the naked eye, so people were trying to learn about structures they could not even see! Even the most powerful **microscopes** available today can only just make out the shape of an atom.

Over the last 100 years or so, scientists have learnt a lot about the structure of the atom, the different particles that are found within it, and how they interact. During these studies some surprising discoveries have been made – and the story of the atom is not complete even now. As we learn more, our understanding of atoms is still changing.

The essence of matter

The story of the discovery of the atom begins almost 2,500 years ago, in ancient Greece. Greek **philosophers** studied the world around them and spent many hours discussing ideas with their fellow philosophers. The Greek philosopher Empedocles (c. 492–432 BC) suggested that all **matter** was made up of four elements – fire, air, water, and earth. Objects were composed of varying amounts of each of these elements. For example, a rock was made mostly of earth, while a living **organism** was largely water and fire. Empedocles' theory was popular, but nobody could find evidence of these four elements.

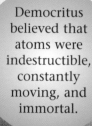

Democritus believed that atoms were indestructible, constantly moving, and immortal.

The philosopher Democritus (c. 450–370 BC) developed his own theory of matter. He asked an important question: "What would happen if you cut an object such as a stone in half again and again?" Democritus believed that eventually you would end up with something so tiny that it could no longer be divided. He called these tiny pieces of matter "atoms", which means "indivisible". He believed that atoms could not be destroyed. He thought that there were different types of atom, each one specific to a particular material.

Democritus vs. Aristotle

Aristotle (384–322 BC) was one of the most influential philosophers of the time – and he thought that Democritus' theory of the atom was all wrong. He believed that if matter was made up of tiny particles then there must be spaces between the particles.

These spaces were empty, which meant that there was a **vacuum**. He did not believe that a vacuum could exist in nature, and therefore he thought Democritus must be incorrect.

Aristotle modified Empedocles' ideas about the four elements to create his own theory of matter, in which the four elements could be transformed into one another. Many other philosophers followed Aristotle's lead and ignored the work of Democritus. More than 2,000 years would pass before many scientists took Democritus' work seriously again.

WHAT WERE THE FOUR ELEMENTS?

The ancient Greeks believed that matter was made up four elements – air, earth, fire, and water. All matter was a mixture of the four elements. For example, when a piece of wood burnt, it showed the four elements – the flames of the fire, the smoke of air, water that bubbled out, and the earthy ash that was left behind.

Empedocles and Aristotle believed everything was made up of four elements – air, earth, fire, and water.

The alchemists

Aristotle believed that each of the four elements could be changed into other elements through a process called **transmutation**. This idea was investigated by people known as **alchemists**. They carried out lots of experiments in their attempts to turn everyday metals such as lead into valuable gold and silver.

Alchemy was widely practised in the Middle East during the 3rd century AD. By the 12th century, alchemists could be found all across Europe, especially in Spain. In England, the first known alchemist was Roger Bacon (c. 1214–1294). He was a great scholar and made discoveries in the fields of astronomy and physics as well as chemistry. He carried out many experiments, but he never managed to discover the Philosopher's Stone (see page 9). By the 14th century, alchemy had fallen into disrepute as many alchemists were con men who tricked people out of their money.

There were many exaggerated stories about Roger Bacon, including one that said he was a powerful sorcerer.

TALKING SCIENCE

The early alchemists used a wide range of chemicals, and gave them exotic names:

Latin name	Common name
cinnabar	mercury (II) chloride or mercury (II) sulphide
spiritus fumans	tin (IV) chloride
saccharum saturni	lead acetate
sal ammoniac	ammonium chloride
oil of vitriol	sulphuric acid
aqua regia	hydrochloric acid
aqua fortis	nitric acid

Many people considered alchemists to be sinister people. They hid themselves away in secret laboratories, where they boiled up liquids in large flasks. They wrote down their findings using coded symbols so that nobody else could steal their ideas.

The Philosopher's Stone
One of the aims of the alchemists was to find the so-called Philosopher's Stone. This was a legendary substance that they thought could change any metal to gold. Some alchemists believed that it was a potion that would make a person immortal. Although the alchemists were never successful, they did make some useful discoveries. For example, they found chemicals such as nitric acid and sulphuric acid. They also worked out how to extract metal from rocks (a process called refining), how to work metal, how to make dyes and inks, how to tan leather, and how to make glass.

This representation of an alchemist's laboratory shows the types of flasks that were used to boil up different liquids.

Discovering chemicals

Not all scientists dismissed the idea of alchemy. In the 17th century, one of the greatest scientists of the time was Robert Boyle (1627–1691). He believed that alchemy could help him understand how **matter** was put together. Boyle was a very religious man. He believed if he could find the Philosopher's Stone he would be able to talk to the spirits of the dead.

Robert Boyle was a leading scientist of his time. He carefully recorded the results of all his experiments. This is the front page of one of his books.

THE
SCEPTICAL CHYMIST:
OR
CHYMICO-PHYSICAL
Doubts & Paradoxes,
Touching the
SPAGYRIST'S PRINCIPLES
Commonly call'd
HYPOSTATICAL;
As they are wont to be Propos'd and Defended by the Generality of
ALCHYMISTS.
Whereunto is præmis'd Part of another Discourse relating to the same Subject.

BY
The Honourable ROBERT BOYLE, Esq;

LONDON,
Printed by J. Cadwell for J. Crooke, and are to be Sold at the Ship in St. Paul's Church-Yard.
MDCLXI.

Boyle was a brilliant scientist and he advanced the understanding of the chemical **elements**. Boyle did not believe that there were just four elements. He thought that the atomistic theory of Democritus was closer to the truth – and he set out to prove it by carrying out a series of chemical experiments.

Primary particles

In 1661, Boyle published *The Sceptical Chymist*, in which he attacked Aristotle's theory of the four elements. He put forward his own theory of "primary particles and corpuscles". In this, he stated that matter was made up of "corpuscles", which were themselves made up of different combinations of what he called "primary particles".

WHAT IS THE LITMUS TEST?

It was Robert Boyle who devised the litmus test for acids and alkalis – the same test that is used today. He noticed that acids turned a particular vegetable indicator from blue to red, while alkalis turned the indicator from red to blue. He found that some substances had no effect on the colour of the indicator. He described these as neutral substances.

He likened the primary particles to tiny **croquet** balls. A croquet ball moves in a certain direction at a certain speed because it has been hit by another croquet ball, which was also moving in a particular direction and at a certain speed. In the same way, the primary particles moved around because they had been bumped by other primary particles.

Boyle believed that the number and organization of the primary particles created the different substances. He suggested that pure substances were made up of the same type of primary particles. These pure substances were elements. There were many different elements, and each one contained a different type of primary particle with unique characteristics. The elements could be joined together to make new substances.

Boyle's experiments

Boyle was one of the first scientists to perform carefully controlled experiments. Just like the **alchemists**, Boyle recorded his findings using symbols and codes. However, he published his research, giving details of his procedures, the equipment he used, and all the observations that he made. He loved to carry out tests to detect the presence of various chemicals. He worked out that he could use ammonia to test for the presence of copper, and silver nitrate to test for salt in water.

These bottles contain indicator chemicals. An acid turns blue litmus paper red, an alkali turns red litmus paper blue.

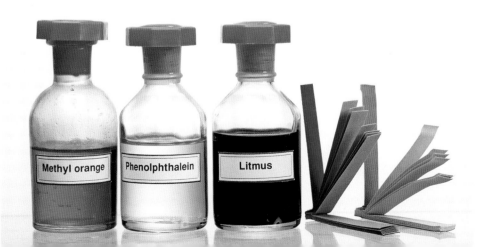

Methyl orange   Phenolphthalein   Litmus

Experiments with gases

Robert Boyle knew that some elements existed as gases while others were liquids or solids. He decided that the primary particles in gases were able to move very freely. In a gas, the primary particles stayed quite far away from each other. The primary particles in liquids were closer to each other but could still move quite freely. Those found in solids were packed so tightly they could not move around.

In 1662, Boyle and his assistant Robert Hooke carried out a series of experiments on gases. They used a J-shaped piece of glass tubing that was sealed at one end. Air was trapped in the sealed end of the tube by a column of the liquid metal mercury. They carefully increased or decreased the pressure and measured the **volume** of gas. At the same time, they made sure that the quantity of gas and the temperature were kept constant. When they increased the pressure above normal **atmospheric pressure**, the volume of the gas decreased, but when they lowered the pressure, the volume increased.

This drawing shows Robert Boyle in his laboratory talking with Denis Papin, a French physicist. Papin is pointing to Boyle's air pump.

Boyle's Law

Boyle's research had shown that pressure was a **force** caused by the movement of particles. When they collided with each other and with the walls of the container, they exerted a force. When the volume was increased, the particles were more widely spaced and there were fewer collisions with the walls. This meant that the gas pressure was less. However, when the volume of gas was decreased, the particles were pushed together and there were more collisions with the wall of the container, so the pressure went up.

As a result of these experiments, Boyle was able to formulate his famous gas law, known as Boyle's Law. This law states that if the temperature is kept the same, the volume of a gas is inversely proportional to the pressure (so, for example, if the pressure is doubled, the volume shrinks by half).

This can has had all the air sucked out of it by a vacuum pump.

WHAT IS A VACUUM PUMP?

One of Boyle's many contributions to science was the invention of the **vacuum** pump. This was a simple piece of apparatus that could suck the air out of a container to create an artificial vacuum. Using his vacuum pump, Boyle was able to show that a reduction in pressure reduced the boiling point of a liquid. At normal atmospheric pressure water boils at 100 °Celsius (212 °Fahrenheit). But when the air pressure was reduced to one-tenth of normal pressure by sucking out some of the air, the water boiled at just 46 °Celsius (115 °Fahrenheit).

Size, shape, and spaces

Another scientist to reject Aristotle's theory of the four elements was a Frenchman, Pierre Gassendi (1592–1655). Gassendi was a deeply religious man and in 1616 he became a priest. He had read about Democritus' theory. He was sure this was correct and that Aristotle was wrong. However, at the time it was very dangerous to hold such views. In 1624, the Parliament of Paris had issued a law that said anyone teaching against the ideas of Aristotle could be put to death. Fortunately, Gassendi had powerful friends, so he was left alone.

Pierre Gassendi was one of the first European scientists to reject the ideas of Aristotle. He wrote a book that influenced a number of English scientists of the time, including Isaac Newton, Robert Boyle, and Robert Hooke.

In 1658, three years after his death, his book *Syntagma Philosophiae Epicuri* was published, in which he set out his theory about the nature of matter. He stated that atoms could not be created or destroyed, that they were solid and had **mass**, and could not be subdivided. However, he made one major change to Democritus' theory. Democritus' theory said that the atoms were immortal so they could not be destroyed. Gassendi stated that atoms had been created by God.

WHAT IS A VACUUM?

The word vacuum means "empty" and it refers to a volume of space that is empty of any matter. Much of space is empty of matter and this is an example of a natural vacuum. However, during the 17th century the idea that there were voids or vacuums between atoms was fiercely debated. Many people believed that it was impossible to have a natural vacuum and that the atoms continually moved around to prevent a void from forming. The atomists believed that vacuums were completely natural. One of the reasons for developing the vacuum pump was to prove that it was possible to create a vacuum.

Halley's comet is named after the astronomer Edmund Halley. In October 1689, he presented a scientific paper on the size of gold atoms. He worked out that an atom of gold had to be less than 0.00019 millimetres (0.0000074 inches) in diameter.

The space between atoms

Gassendi tried to explain how the shape of the atoms could influence the behaviour of different substances. For example, he suggested that the atoms in water were smooth so that water could flow, while atoms in iron had little hooks that linked them together to form a hard, strong metal. Lightweight substances contained loosely packed atoms with empty spaces or voids between them (a vacuum). He also stated that the atoms could group together to form *moleculae* (**molecules**) or *corpusculae* (corpuscles).

Atoms and elements

In the 18th century, Aristotle's theory of the four elements was finally disproved. The breakthrough came when the Englishman Joseph Priestley (1733–1804) and the Frenchman Antoine Lavoisier (1743–1794) showed that two of the four **elements** – air and water – were not elements at all, but substances made up of combinations of elements.

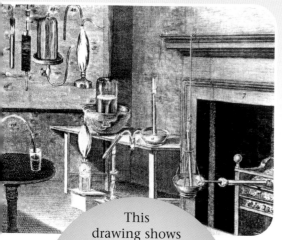

This drawing shows the apparatus that was used by Joseph Priestley in his gas experiments. He discovered 10 gases, including oxygen, hydrogen chloride, nitrous oxide, and sulphur dioxide.

Joseph Priestley was a religious man who became a minister in Leeds in England. While visiting a brewery, he noticed that the **fermenting** barley grains that were being used to make beer were producing a gas. This sparked his interest, and he carried out some experiments. He found that the gas was so dense that it sank to the floor of the room. Also, the gas could be used to put out flames. The gas was carbon dioxide, but Priestley did not know this at the time.

Experiments with plants

Some time later, Priestley discovered that plants produced the same gas when they were kept in the dark. In 1771, he showed that when a plant shoot was placed in a glass jar with a burning candle, the gas produced by the shoot put out the flame.

THAT'S AMAZING!

In the 17th century, scientists believed that in all material that could be burned there was a substance called phlogiston. It was this colourless, odourless, tasteless, and weightless substance that was given off in burning. Of course, this is not true, but Joseph Priestley was a strong believer in the phlogiston theory, and the theory led scientists astray for a long time.

When Priestley dissolved carbon dioxide gas in water, he discovered that it gave the water a sweet acidic taste. He named this "soda water", which he described as a refreshing drink, and he sold it to his friends. He found he could make large amounts of carbon dioxide by dripping sulphuric acid on to chalk. Don't try this at home!

Priestley then found that if he left the shoot in the jar in the light for several days, he could relight the candle and it continued to burn. He concluded that the plant had produced a different gas that allowed the candle to burn.

The following year, Priestley carried out one of his best-known experiments, in which he placed a mouse in a sealed jar until it collapsed. However, if the mouse was placed in a jar with a plant, it survived. He concluded that the plant had produced an important gas that the mouse needed in order to survive. Further experiments in 1774 led him to the conclusion that this "good air" made up about 20 per cent of atmospheric air.

Joseph Priestley is most famous for discovering carbon dioxide.

Meeting with Lavoisier

Priestley travelled to France, where he met the French chemist Antoine Lavoisier. He told Lavoisier how he had made this "good air". This was the clue that Lavoisier needed to complete some of his own research. He showed that this gas was essential in burning. He decided to call the gas oxygen. Priestley and Lavoisier had proved that air was in fact made up of several gases and so it could not be an element. They had shown beyond doubt that Aristotle's theory about elements was wrong.

Lavoisier was a high-ranking government official and was accused of being a traitor in 1794, during the French Revolution. He was tried, convicted, and guillotined on the same day. After his death he was found to be completely innocent.

The conservation of matter

Lavoisier and his wife carried out a series of experiments in which they burnt elements such as phosphorus and sulphur in air. He carefully weighed the **reactants** and all the products – something that had not been done before. He found that the quantity of **matter** at the beginning of a reaction was the same as at the end, but that it had been rearranged into different substances. As a result, Lavoisier came up with his theory of the conservation of matter. In this, he stated that "matter is neither created nor destroyed, but is changed from one form to another". This was a turning point in our understanding of the nature of matter.

In addition to this, Lavoisier explained that an element was a simple substance that could not be broken down by any known method of chemical analysis. He explained how chemical **compounds** could be made from elements. He was the first scientist to put together a list of elements, which included oxygen, nitrogen, hydrogen, phosphorus, mercury, zinc, and sulphur. However, Lavoisier didn't get everything right – he also included light, which he mistakenly believed to be an element.

Another of Lavoisier's great achievements was developing the metric system so that the same weights and measures could be used throughout France. He was executed at the age of 51, but during his lifetime he had made several important contributions to the development of science.

WHO DISCOVERED OXYGEN?

In 1772, the Swedish chemist Carl Wilhelm Scheele (1742–1786) discovered the gas oxygen. However, Joseph Priestley – who discovered oxygen in 1774 – published his findings three years before Scheele released his paper. Antoine Lavoisier was the first scientist to describe oxygen as an element, and was the first to give it its name, a word that comes from the Greek word meaning "acid-former".

Dalton's theories

Atomic theory was developed even further by John Dalton (1766–1844). He had read the work of scientists such as Antoine Lavoisier and developed his own theory. In 1808, Dalton published *New System of Chemical Philosophy*. The five main points of his atomic theory were:

- Elements are made of tiny particles called atoms.

- All atoms of a particular element are identical.

- The atoms of a given element are different from those of any other element.

- Atoms of one element can combine with atoms of other elements to form compounds. (For example, water is made by a hydrogen atom joining to an oxygen atom.)

- Atoms cannot be created, divided into smaller particles, or destroyed in the chemical process. A chemical reaction simply changes the way atoms are grouped together.

One of the gases that Dalton experimented with was marsh gas, which contained methane. He collected the marsh gas from waterlogged areas, where there was lots of rotting vegetation. The gas was released by the vegetation and became trapped in the mud. When Dalton disturbed the mud with a stick, the gas was released and he could capture it in an upturned jar.

Amazingly, much of Dalton's atomic theory has been proved to be correct. Only three parts have been partially disproved by modern science.

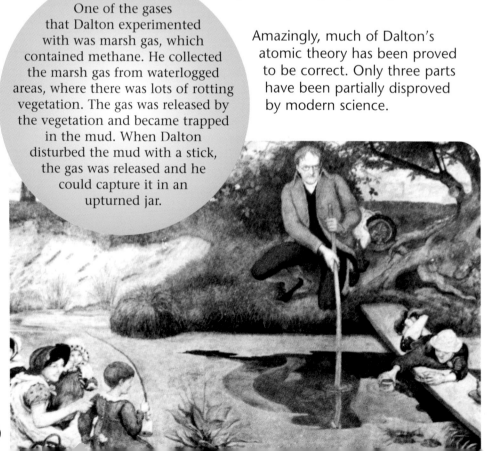

Dalton believed that when atoms combined, it was usually one to one. This gave the chemical formula for water as OH – that is, one atom of oxygen joined to one of hydrogen. In fact, water is made up of two hydrogen atoms and one oxygen atom, and its chemical formula is H_2O.

ELEMENTS

	wt		wt
Hydrogen.	1	Strontian	46
Azote	5	Barytes	68
Carbon	54	Iron	50
Oxygen	7	Zinc	56
Phosphorus	9	Copper	56
Sulphur	13	Lead	90
Magnesia	20	Silver	190
Lime	24	Gold	190
Soda	28	Platina	190
Potash	42	Mercury	167

This is John Dalton's table of elements, with their relative atomic mass and the symbols he used to represent each element. This version was published in 1803.

Dalton made a similar mistake with ammonia, believing it to be NH rather than NH_3. What is more, we now know that atoms can in fact be split, and this is the basis of nuclear energy (see page 44). Also, not all the atoms in a particular element are identical – we now know that some elements have **isotopes** (see page 46).

Atomic mass

Another of Dalton's great achievements was to put together a table that listed the relative **mass** of atoms. His first table was published in 1803 and improved in 1808. It listed 20 substances he thought were elements, although some were in fact compounds (for example, lime). Dalton gave the relative mass of a number of atoms, which he had worked out from analysing substances such as water, ammonia, and carbon dioxide. He calculated the mass of each element relative to hydrogen, which he knew to be the lightest atom. The heaviest in his list was mercury, although scientists now know that lead has a larger relative mass.

WHAT IS ATOMIC MASS?

Atomic mass is the mass of a single atom of an element. It is measured in units in which an atom of carbon weighs exactly 12. On this scale, the atomic mass of hydrogen is approximately 1, that of helium is 4, and so on.

Molecules and the periodic table

One thing Dalton had been unable to work out was how many atoms there were in a **molecule**. For example, he guessed that a water molecule had one atom of hydrogen and one of oxygen, which was wrong. This problem was solved when scientists figured out how to weigh atoms. It was Italian scientist Amedeo Avogadro (1776–1856) who took the next step.

Observing gases

Avogadro believed that gases such as hydrogen and oxygen could never exist as individual atoms. Instead, he thought they occurred in pairs, as molecules. However, because this idea went against the findings of Dalton – which were highly respected – many scientists ignored his suggestion.

In 1811, Avogadro suggested that equal **volumes** of gases, if kept at the same temperature and pressure, would contain the same number of molecules. He carried out experiments using gases such as nitrogen, hydrogen, oxygen, and chlorine.

Avogadro studied law at university. However, he had always been interested in science, so he decided to give up law and study mathematics and physics instead.

He noticed that when the temperature and pressure were kept the same, the gases combined in a particular way. For example, 1 litre (0.22 gallons) of nitrogen combined with 3 litres (0.66 gallons) of hydrogen to form ammonia (NH_3), and 2 litres (0.44 gallons) of hydrogen combined with 1 litre (0.22 gallons) of oxygen to form water (H_2O). The next step was to weigh the gases. He found that a litre of oxygen weighed 16 times more than a litre of hydrogen. Therefore an oxygen atom must be 16 times the **mass** of a hydrogen atom. He weighed lots of different gases and was able to work out a scale of relative masses. Hydrogen atoms had the least mass.

Avogadro's number

The number of molecules in equal volumes of gases later became known as Avogadro's number. Unfortunately, few scientists paid much attention to this idea, and Avogadro died before there was proof that his theory was correct. In 1860, the Italian chemist Stanislao Cannizzaro published a series of about 60 atomic masses that he had discovered using Avogadro's hypothesis, showing that it could be applied to solids as well as gases.

It was another 80 years, though, before Avogadro's number would be worked out. Avogadro's number (now called Avogadro's Constant) corresponds to the number of atoms or molecules needed to make up a mass equal to the substance's atomic or molecular mass, in grams. For example, the atomic mass of carbon-12 is 12, so Avogadro's number of carbon-12 atoms (i.e. one **mole** of carbon atoms) has a mass of 12 grams (0.4 ounces). Eventually, Avogadro's number was calculated to be 6×10^{23} molecules per **gram-mole**.

Each of these beakers of coloured compounds contains Avogadro's number of molecules.

WHO WAS CANNIZZARO?

Italian Stanislao Cannizzaro was one of the few chemists who decided to apply Avogadro's theory to find out the mass of different gas molecules. In doing so, he proved Avogadro to be right. Cannizzaro showed that atomic mass could be linked to the structure of chemical **compounds**. He worked out the atomic mass for the 60 or so elements that were known to exist in the 1860s.

The periodic table

Stanislao Cannizzaro had created a table of 60 or so **elements** in order of their relative molecular masses. Several chemists, including Beguyer de Chancourtois and John Newlands, had tried to group the elements according to their behaviour, but they had been unsuccessful. It was the Russian Dmitri Mendeleev (1834–1907) who finally created the basis of the periodic table we are familiar with today.

In 1869, Mendeleev created a table that listed all the known elements in order of increasing atomic mass. He called it the periodic table. He noticed that if he organized the elements into rows rather than in a single column, a pattern emerged. However, this pattern only worked properly if he left gaps in the table. The idea of leaving gaps in the table and predicting what the missing elements might be was a great breakthrough. When gallium was discovered, Mendeleev was proved right – so people accepted the rest of his ideas.

Mendeleev put together his periodic table by writing out the names of all the known elements on cards. He arranged the cards in columns in order of atomic weight. He didn't know what to do with hydrogen, the lightest element, so he left it out.

TALKING SCIENCE

"I began to look about and write down the elements with their atomic weights and typical properties, analogous elements and like atomic weights on separate cards, and this soon convinced me that the properties of elements are in periodic dependence upon their atomic weights."
Dmitri Mendeleev, *Principles of Chemistry*, Vol. II, 1905

Groups of elements

Mendeleev had discovered that elements with similar properties appeared in the same vertical column of the table. This meant that they could also have similar structures. For example, the first column of the table contained the Group I elements, including sodium and potassium. They were all silvery-coloured metals. They were all soft and could be cut with a knife to expose a shiny surface that quickly tarnished in air. They all reacted with water to produce hydrogen gas. By arranging the elements in rows, it was possible to predict the existence of undiscovered elements.

Since Mendeleev's time there have been a number of changes to the periodic table. For example, the group known as the noble gases was not on Mendeleev's table because they had not been discovered. The modern periodic table is made up of 90 naturally occurring elements and 25 elements that are made in the laboratory. Some of the relative molecular masses have been revised and some elements have been given different positions, but essentially the table is the same as in 1871.

WHAT IS GALLIUM?

One of the gaps in the periodic table was filled by the metal gallium. It was discovered by the Frenchman Lecoq de Boisbaudran in 1875. This is one of only four metals that are liquid at room temperature (the others are mercury, caesium, and rubidium). It is liquid over a wide range of temperatures, so it can be used in thermometers that measure very high temperatures. When it is painted on glass, it creates a mirror.

Gallium is used in light-emitting diodes (LEDs) that produce a blue light.

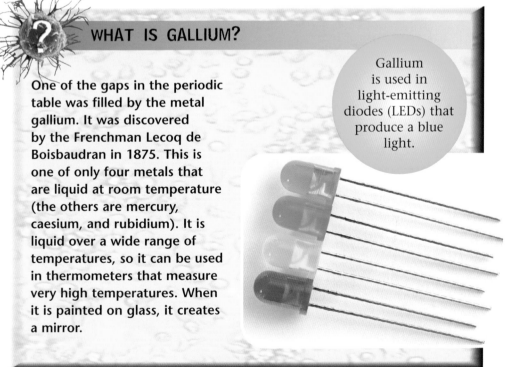

Moving atoms

During the second half of the 19th century, scientists learned more about the way in which atoms and molecules in a gas move around. The key scientists working between 1860 and 1890 were the Scottish physicist James Clerk Maxwell (1831–1879) and the Austrian physicist Ludwig Boltzmann (1844–1906). Their research resulted in the kinetic theory of movement of atoms and molecules.

Colliding molecules

James Clerk Maxwell's interest in the movement of gases had been sparked by his studies of astronomy. He had seen the rings of Saturn through a telescope and was intrigued by the way particles moved through the rings. At the time, most scientists believed that all the molecules in a gas travelled at the same speed, but Maxwell thought differently. He believed that the molecules in a gas were continually moving around in a random way, bumping into each other as they did so. When the molecules collided, they slowed each other down. In order to work out the speed at which the gas could travel, Maxwell needed to calculate the speeds of all the different molecules. He devised a formula, which is now known as Maxwell's Distribution. Ludwig Boltzmann read about Maxwell's work. He ended up modifying Maxwell's formula to explain how gas molecules conducted heat.

Maxwell's ideas of how molecules moved around came from his observations of the rings of Saturn.

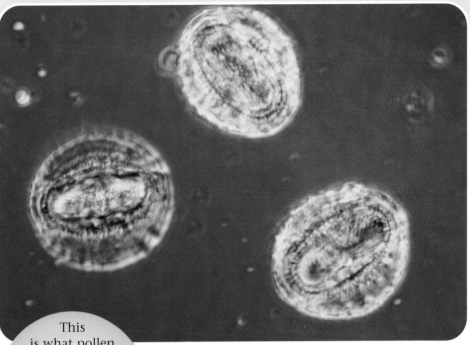

This is what pollen grains look like, magnified more than 1,000 times, when viewed through a light microscope.

Brownian motion

More clues to how atoms moved around came from a chance observation by English botanist Robert Brownian in 1827. He was using a **microscope** to look at pollen grains floating on water. He saw that the grains were not still – they kept on jiggling around in all directions. Surprised by this, he decided they must be alive. However, when he looked at dust under the microscope, he saw a similar movement – but he had no idea what caused it. This movement became known as Brownian motion.

? WHAT CAUSED BROWNIAN MOTION?

It was Albert Einstein (1879–1955) who finally explained Brownian motion. In 1905, he published a number of papers. In one of them, he explained that the pollen grains moved because the water molecules around them were moving. Although the pollen grains were about 1,000 times larger than the water molecules, there were far more water molecules. The water molecules were moving around and bumping into the pollen grains from all directions. When enough of them bumped into the same pollen grain, they caused it to move.

Into the atom

By the end of the 19th century, scientists knew that there were atoms and **molecules**. They imagined atoms to be like tiny, indestructible **billiard** balls. Imagine their surprise when they discovered that atoms were made up of even smaller particles.

The astounding discovery was made in 1897 by the Englishman Joseph John Thomson (1856–1940), who was working at the University of Cambridge. Thomson was one of several scientists who were experimenting with a new piece of apparatus – a glass tube from which all the air had been sucked, called a cathode ray tube. At one end was a metal cathode (the negative **electrode**) and at the other was an anode (positive electrode). When electricity was passed through the metal cathode, it sent out a stream of particles that were attracted to the anode. Thompson was trying to work out the nature of these particles.

J. J. Thomson was the first person to realize that there must be something inside atoms – they were not indivisible after all.

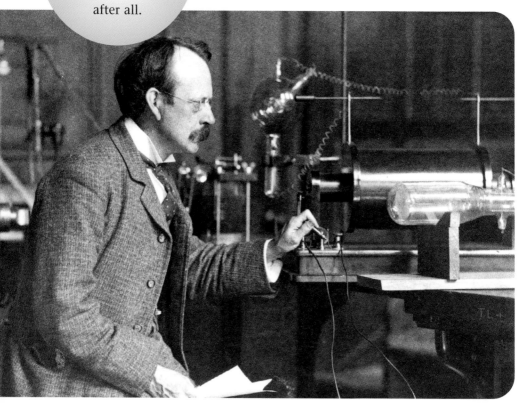

Thomson's electrons

As a result of his investigations, Thomson concluded that the beam was made up of really tiny particles, each one about 1,800 times smaller than an atom. What was so startling about this was that these particles had to be parts of atoms. This went against the long-held theory that atoms were indivisible. These particles became known as electrons, and they carried a small negative electrical charge.

This is an early cathode ray tube. When an electric current is passed through the cathode, a beam of electrons is produced and they travel in a straight line. They cast a shadow of the metal cross shape on to the glass screen.

In 1904, Thomson announced his ideas about the structure of the atom. He believed that an atom was a sphere made up of positively charged **matter**. Held inside the sphere by the positive charges were negatively charged electrons. This became known as the "plum pudding" model, as the electrons were scattered around the atom like plums in a pudding.

? WHAT IS A CATHODE RAY TUBE?

Cathode ray tubes are so named because they emit a ray of electrons from the cathode. Scientists found that they could focus the beam to make an image on a screen – which led to the invention of television. The cathode ray tube in early televisions consisted of a glass **vacuum** tube containing a heated filament. An electric current heated up the filament, causing it to emit a beam of electrons. The beam was focused by an electromagnet so that it hit a flat screen at the other end of the tube. The screen was coated with a layer of phosphor, a substance that glowed when it was hit by the electrons. In a colour television screen there are rows of three types of phosphors, which produce red, green, and blue light.

Discovering protons

Electrons had a negative charge, so scientists now knew that the atom must contain another particle with a positive charge. Early experiments with the cathode ray tube had indicated that there was a beam travelling in the opposite direction to the electrons. This must be made of positively charged particles. But what were those particles?

One of J. J. Thomson's students was a New Zealand-born scientist named Ernest Rutherford (1871–1937), who was investigating how electricity was conducted in gases. When X-rays were discovered (see page 32), Rutherford realized that he could use them in his experiments. In this way, he found that X-rays could make a gas conduct electricity.

Alpha particles

In 1898, Rutherford began to study some of the larger atoms, such as uranium. He found that uranium decayed (broke up) over time and in the process emitted smaller particles. He called them alpha particles and beta rays. Beta rays were found to be high-speed electrons. Although nobody could figure out exactly what the alpha particle was, they did know that it was extremely small. Alpha particles are now known to consist of two protons and two neutrons.

Hans Geiger and Ernest Rutherford working in the laboratory at Manchester University.

In 1911, Rutherford moved to the University of Manchester, UK, where he was helped in his research by two students, Hans Geiger and Ernest Marsden. Rutherford asked Marsden to investigate the effect of alpha particles on metals. Marsden fired alpha particles at thin sheets of gold.

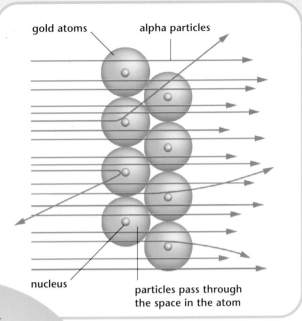

gold atoms · alpha particles

nucleus

particles pass through the space in the atom

Rutherford realized that Thomson's model of the atom was wrong. In fact, an atom was mostly empty space. This meant that most of the alpha particles passed right through. Almost all of the mass of an atom was concentrated in a nucleus located right in the middle. When an alpha particle hit the nucleus it was bounced back. Rutherford likened the atom to a mini solar system, in which the nucleus was the Sun and the electrons were the planets in orbit around it.

A screen was placed behind the gold sheet so that any alpha particles passing through the gold would appear as a flash of light on the screen. The results were surprising. Some alpha particles passed right through the foil on to the screen, but others were reflected off at an angle. It was like firing bullets at a piece of paper, and some of them bouncing off!

Splitting the atom

Further experiments revealed the answer. In 1919 they found the positive charge they had been looking for – they had "split" the atom. Now scientists had evidence that atoms had a **nucleus** surrounded by electrons. For about 20 years, the nucleus was thought to consist of a number of protons equal to the atomic weight. However, there was a growing feeling among scientists that there was something missing.

TALKING SCIENCE

"If, as I have reason to believe, I have disintegrated the nucleus of the atom, this is of greater significance than the war."
Ernest Rutherford, 1919

Discovering neutrons

The missing particle was discovered in 1932 by the British scientist James Chadwick (1891–1974). It was called the neutron because it had no charge. It was found with the protons in the nucleus of the atom.

James Chadwick and several other researchers looking for the missing particle had been puzzled by some of their results. The atomic number of an atom is the number of positive charges, or protons, in the nucleus. Since electrons have almost no **mass**, Chadwick expected that the atomic number would be the same as the atomic mass – but this was not the case. Something was adding to the mass, and it was not the electrons. Chadwick suspected that there could be a particle with mass but no charge. Further experiments revealed the neutron, which had virtually the same mass as the proton but no charge.

HOW DID RÖNTGEN DISCOVER X-RAYS?

This is the first ever X-ray. It shows the bones in the hand of Röntgen's wife.

The German scientist Wilhelm Röntgen (1845–1923) discovered X-rays by accident in 1895, when he was working with a covered cathode ray tube in a darkened room. When the tube was turned on, the beam of electrons caused a paper plate covered in the chemical barium to glow. He put several objects between the tube and the plate and they appeared as a transparent image on the plate. When he asked his wife to place her hand in the beam, an image of the bones in her hand appeared on the plate. Because Röntgen did not know anything about these new rays he called them X-rays. This was the beginning of the study of radioactivity.

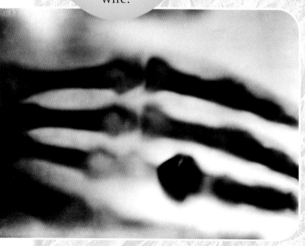

This discovery dramatically altered the model of the atom. Protons and neutrons were found in the nucleus, while electrons orbited the nucleus. The number of protons was equal to the atomic number of the atom.

The useful neutron

This new idea accelerated discoveries in atomic physics. Scientists soon found that the neutron made an ideal "bullet" for bombarding other nuclei. Unlike charged particles, it was not repelled by similarly charged particles. In fact, the neutron could smash right into the nucleus. Soon neutrons were being used to bombard uranium atoms, splitting the nucleus and releasing energy.

Atomic mass and atomic number

- The electrons in an atom have virtually no mass. This means that the mass of an atom is almost all due to the protons and neutrons.

- The mass number is the total number of protons and neutrons in an atom.

- The atomic number is the number of protons in an atom.

For example, carbon has six protons, so its atomic number is six. It also has six neutrons so its mass number is 12. Sometimes the number of neutrons in an atom can vary. Two atoms of the same **element** that contain different numbers of neutrons are called **isotopes**. The atoms have the same atomic number (the number of protons in the nucleus) but different mass numbers because they contain different numbers of neutrons.

This diagram shows the difference between mass number and atomic number.

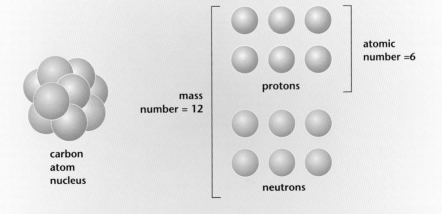

carbon atom nucleus

mass number = 12

protons

atomic number =6

neutrons

Understanding electrons

While people such as James Chadwick were looking for the missing particles of the atom, other scientists were looking at the electrons in more detail. In particular, they wanted to know more about the way electrons moved around the nucleus.

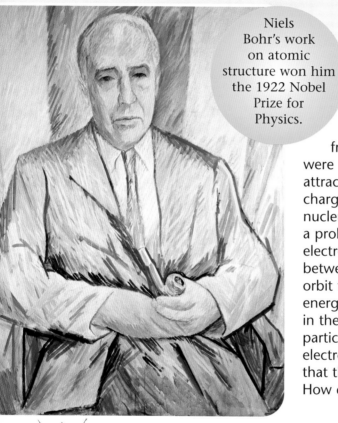

Niels Bohr's work on atomic structure won him the 1922 Nobel Prize for Physics.

In 1911, Rutherford suggested that the electrons were spinning around the **nucleus**, rather like the planets orbiting the Sun. Each electron was a different distance from the nucleus and they were held in their orbits by the attraction of the positive charges of the protons in the nucleus. However, there was a problem with his theory – electrons seemed to move between orbits. As electrons orbit the nucleus, they lose energy. They release this energy in the form of **photons** (light particles). Eventually, the electrons slow down so much that they fall into the nucleus. How could this happen?

THAT'S AMAZING!

The smallest known atom is hydrogen, with a diameter of about 5×10^{-8} millimetres (2×10^{-9} inches). It would take almost 20 million hydrogen atoms to make a line as long as this dash: –. Much of the space taken up by a hydrogen atom is empty because the one electron spins far from the nucleus (which contains one proton). If the atom was the size of a football stadium the nucleus would be the size of a pea.

The importance of light

The Danish physicist Niels Bohr solved the problem in 1913. He had been investigating the behaviour of electrons when they gained and lost energy. In his experiments he passed a current of electricity through a tube filled with gas. When heated by the electricity, electrons in the gas became "excited". When they lost this energy they emitted light. Bohr found that each type of gas emitted a certain colour of light. After studying his results, Bohr suggested that the electrons were arranged in energy levels around the nucleus.

These levels (shells) were arranged in circles around the nucleus. Bohr suggested that each level could only accommodate a certain number of electrons. In his structure of the atom, the innermost electron shell held a maximum of two electrons. If an atom had more than two electrons it had a second electron shell, which had a maximum of eight electrons. If an atom had more than ten electrons it had a third shell, which also had a maximum of eight electrons, and so on.

The evidence for this arrangement of electrons came from the chemical properties of the **elements**. In the 1920s, Bohr and the German scientist Arnold Sommerfeld worked on the atomic structure of elements such as sodium. They concluded that a sodium atom must have a single electron orbiting in the furthest electron shell, while the rest of the electrons were found closer to the nucleus.

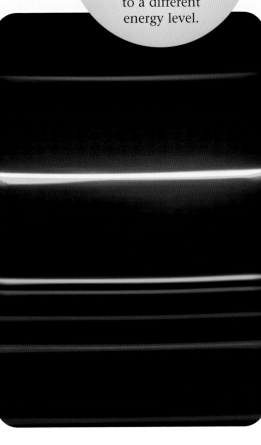

These coloured lights ("spectra") come from the gas helium. Each band of colour corresponds to a specific energy of photon released by electrons jumping to a different energy level.

Electron waves and clouds

The Bohr model of the atom (see page 39) was a big step forwards. Bohr's model of atomic structure was easy to understand and it is the model that is taught in schools today. However, there were still some questions unanswered. Why were electrons confined to certain energy levels? And why didn't electrons emit light all the time?

In 1924, the French scientist Louis de Broglie (1892–1987) realized that light could exist not only as a tiny particle (called a photon) but also as a wave. He suggested that electrons might behave in the same way as light – showing properties of both a particle and a wave. This meant that Bohr's model was not quite right. De Broglie came up with a new model of the atom, in which the electrons moved in their orbits like a wiggly snake. So instead of having a tiny electron orbiting the nucleus, following a circular path, the electron was moving around like a wave.

When a guitar string is plucked it vibrates. These vibrations are waves. As the vibrations pass through air, they produce a sound. De Broglie suggested that electrons moved in waves, too.

Electrons with more energy moved more quickly and had longer **wavelengths**. They were found further from the nucleus. Electrons orbiting nearest to the nucleus had the least energy so had the smallest orbits.

Quantum theory

By the 1920s, physicists had realized that the existing rules used to describe **forces** such as **gravity** could not be applied to atoms. The new rules they devised were called **quantum theory**. In agreeing these new rules, there were lots of debates between scientists from many different countries, including people such as Niels Bohr and the Germans Albert Einstein and Werner Heisenberg. For example, it was suggested that it was impossible to predict the precise moment when an atom would emit a packet, or "quantum" of light. Einstein refused to accept this uncertainty in an atom's behaviour.

Charles Wilson used his cloud chamber to study atomic particles. This invention won him the 1927 Nobel Prize for Physics.

By the late 1920s, Heisenberg published some ideas that would change the rules again. His research showed that it was impossible to predict where an electron was at any one time. He decided that the orbit of an electron was neither a circle nor a wiggle. Instead, it was a cloud covering the area where the electron was most likely to be.

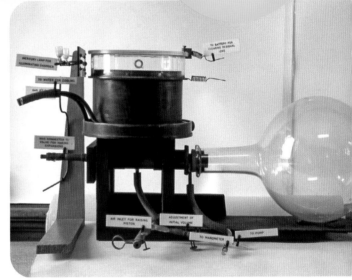

WHAT IS A CLOUD CHAMBER?

In 1912 the Scottish scientist Charles Wilson invented the cloud chamber, which revolutionized the study of atomic particles. He evaporated water in an enclosed chamber to the point that the air was saturated with water vapour. Then he lowered the pressure in the chamber, creating even more water vapour. When a charged particle travelled across the chamber, it caused the vapour to condense into tiny droplets. Although the particle was invisible, it left a characteristic trail in the chamber. An alpha particle left a wide and straight trail of a specific length, while the trail of an electron was a very thin path with lots of twists and turns.

Atomic structure – a summary

By the 1920s, scientists had discovered some of the main particles in atoms, identified about 70 **elements**, and had a good idea of how the protons and electrons were arranged in the atom. They also knew that something must be holding the positively charged protons in the **nucleus**, although it wasn't until 1932 that the neutron was discovered. These are the various models of the atom.

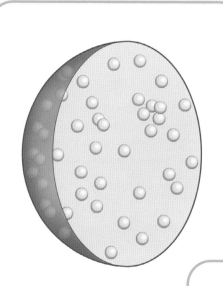

1.
J. J. Thomson
In 1904, Thomson suggested that electrons were found scattered through an atom, like pieces of fruit in a pudding.

2.
Ernest Rutherford
By 1911, Rutherford had discovered that the atom was mostly empty space. The protons were found in the nucleus, while the electrons orbited it.

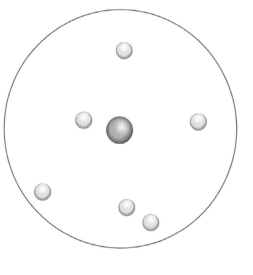

3.
Niels Bohr and Arnold Sommerfeld

This model showed the electrons spinning in specific energy levels (shells). There was a maximum of two electrons in the innermost shell, and eight in the next shells. The number of electrons in the outermost shell contributed to the chemical properties of the element. This shows a carbon atom, with two electrons in the first shell and four in the outer shell. With the addition of neutrons in the nucleus, this structure is the same as the one taught in schools.

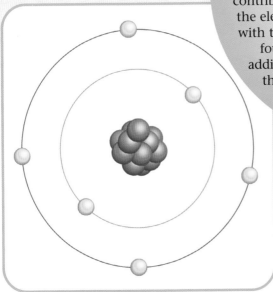

4.
Louis de Broglie

In 1924, De Broglie visualized the electrons as waves circling the nucleus. This shows a hydrogen atom, with a single electron orbiting the nucleus, which contains one proton.

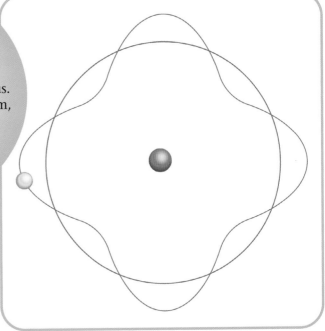

Discovering antimatter

Soon after scientists had agreed that electrons were negatively charged and protons were positively charged, another scientist suggested that there must be also be some positively charged electrons.

Dirac's equation won him a Nobel Prize in 1933. In his Nobel Lecture, he told the audience that there could be another universe – the mirror of our own Universe – made out of antimatter!

In 1928, British scientist Paul Dirac (1902–1984) calculated that there should be a positive electron. He had devised a mathematical equation to describe the behaviour of an electron. This proved confusing, because the equation could have two solutions – one for an electron with positive energy, and one for an electron with negative energy.

Dirac concluded that for every particle that exists there is a corresponding **antiparticle**. The antiparticle matches the particle in every way but one – it has an opposite charge. For every negatively charged electron, for example, there is an opposite electron with a positive charge. This was an astonishing development. The hunt for these mysterious antiparticles soon began.

? WHERE HAS ALL THE ANTIMATTER GONE?

Dirac's equation states that for every particle there is an antiparticle, which is created at the same time. However, when a particle and its corresponding antiparticle come together, they **annihilate** (destroy) each other and energy is released. Scientists believe that at the beginning of the Universe, at the time of the **Big Bang**, there was slightly more **matter** than **antimatter**. Within seconds, most of the antimatter had been wiped out, leaving a small amount of matter that created the Universe as we know it.

This is an image of our own galaxy – the Milky Way. The picture was taken by the Cosmic Background Explorer (COBE), which studies cosmic background radiation.

Cosmic rays

At the start of the 20th century, scientists were investigating a puzzling phenomenon. There was more **radiation** in the atmosphere than could come from natural background radioactivity. In 1912, the Austrian scientist Victor Hess (1883–1964) took a simple device for measuring radiation on a balloon flight. He took a dangerous journey to a point where there was no oxygen in the atmosphere. As his balloon rose, the amount of radiation increased – it was coming from outer space. This became known as cosmic radiation. It consists of high-energy particles that give out a lot of energy when they are involved in reactions.

In 1932, Carl Anderson (1905–1991), a professor at the California Institute of Technology in the USA, was using a cloud chamber to study showers of cosmic particles. He found something unusual – a track left by something that was positively charged. It had the same **mass** as an electron. He spent many hours studying these tracks, trying to work out what they were. Finally he came to the conclusion that the tracks were actually antielectrons. The impact of the cosmic rays in the cloud chamber had created both an electron and an antielectron. He called the antielectron a **positron**. For many years, cosmic rays remained the only source of high-energy particles. Lots of other discoveries were made, but it was 22 years before the **antiproton** was found.

Holding the nucleus together

The positive charge of the protons in the **nucleus** attracted the negative charge of the electrons. This meant that the electrons could be held in place as they orbited the nucleus. However, scientists still did not understand what was holding the protons in the nucleus. Since all the protons had positive charges, they should repel each other. There had to be a **force** like a magnet holding the particles in the nucleus together.

At the time, scientists only knew about two forces – **gravity** and electric force. Gravity is the force of attraction between two bodies. However, this could not be the force in the nucleus of an atom because gravity only has a noticeable effect when large objects, such as planets, are involved. Electric force is the force that exists between particles of opposite charge, such as the proton and the electron. Another force was holding the protons and neutrons together.

Strong nuclear force

When James Chadwick discovered the neutron in 1932, he suggested that there was a very strong force in the nucleus that held all the protons and neutrons together. We now know that the nuclear force is about 100 times stronger than the repulsive force that exists between the protons.

WHAT ARE NEUTRINOS?

Neutrinos are very tiny, high-energy particles. They can pass easily through **matter** and are very difficult to detect. They are produced by many events in space and they travel quickly through space. They can be used in the same way that light is used to see objects. One particular use is to study **supernovae**. These are the huge explosions that take place when a star comes to the end of its life. The energy is released in a stream of neutrinos that travel out across space. Neutrinos may help astronomers to see our Solar System more clearly.

In 1934, the Japanese scientist Hideki Yukawa (1907–1981) tried to explain how the nuclear force worked. He predicted that it resulted from the exchange of a particle between the neutrons and the protons. He named the particle a **meson**. Over the next few years, American scientists observed these particles in the laboratory. In 1947, the English scientist Cecil Powell (1903–1969) observed mesons in the upper atmosphere, where they were produced by cosmic-ray collisions. This type of meson was called a pion and it had a **mass** 70 times that of an electron. Since then, a number of different types of meson have been found – and they have been given some strange-sounding names! The pion is one of the smallest, while among the largest is the kaon. This has a mass greater than a proton.

A few years later, the Italian scientist Enrico Fermi (1901–1954) showed that there was another, weaker, force acting in the nucleus, which made protons split into neutrons, electrons, and **neutrinos**.

This is a small part of a supernova that exploded about 15,000 years ago. The bluish ribbon of light stretching left to right could be gas ejected by the supernova. Events like this release streams of the high-energy particles called neutrinos.

Atom power

The 1930s and 1940s were very exciting times for scientists working on atoms. Discoveries were being made all the time, and one of the most important of these was **nuclear fission**.

The first steps towards nuclear fission were made in 1928, when the British scientist John Cockcroft teamed up with the Irish scientist Ernest Walton at Cambridge University to study protons. In 1932, they bombarded the **element** lithium with high-energy protons, and succeeded in changing it into helium and other chemical elements.

The discovery of the neutron in 1932 enabled other scientists to take a step forwards. One of these scientists was the Italian Enrico Fermi, who was investigating the **forces** that held the **nucleus** together. In 1934, he found that he could split uranium atoms by bombarding them with neutrons. What was unexpected was that the splitting of the uranium atom was accompanied by the release of a lot of energy.

In 1939, the German scientists Otto Hahn and Fritz Strassman proved that uranium could be split to form elements such as barium, which is about half the **mass** of uranium.

The natural decay of uranium is sped up by bombarding the uranium with neutrons. A neutron sticks to a nucleus, the way a magnet sticks to a lump of steel. This is enough to destabilize the uranium atom and cause it to break up.

three more neutrons released

energy

neutron

nucleus of a large atom

atom splits

two smaller atoms

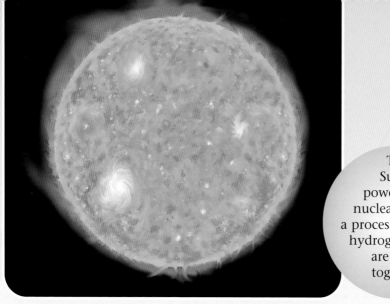

The Sun is powered by nuclear fusion, a process by which hydrogen atoms are fused together.

The Austrians Lise Meitner and her nephew Otto Frisch studied all the available evidence and came up with the theory of nuclear fission. In this, the neutron was taken up by the nucleus of the uranium atom. This caused the nucleus to become unstable and split into two unequal parts, releasing large quantities of energy.

Nuclear fission

In nature, uranium is a large atom with 92 protons. Its nuclei are unstable. Over very long periods of time, they slowly decay, emitting alpha and beta particles. When uranium emits an alpha particle, its nucleus loses two protons. This means that it is no longer uranium. It has changed into thorium. This process of decay continues for millions of years. Eventually the uranium will have turned into lead.

WHAT IS NUCLEAR FUSION?

The Sun is powered by a nuclear process known as **nuclear fusion** – the opposite to nuclear fission. In the core of the Sun, where temperatures reach about 15 million °Celsius (27 million °Fahrenheit), hydrogen atoms are fused together to form helium. This reaction generates enough energy to keep the Sun burning. Almost all the helium used to fill balloons and for other uses is extracted from rocks and natural gas. The source of the helium is the alpha particles from the decay of uranium over millions of years.

Electricity vs. bombs

During the late 1930s, Niels Bohr carried out some experiments on a rare **isotope** of uranium, called uranium-235. This has 92 protons and 143 neutrons, while the more common form of uranium, U-238, has 92 protons and 146 neutrons. Bohr discovered that a neutron was one of the products of nuclear fission. He had a brilliant idea. He visualized a chain reaction in which the neutrons created by the splitting of the first uranium atom would collide with, and split, more uranium atoms. It would be a self-sustaining reaction that would release vast amounts of energy.

Bohr travelled to Washington in the United States to discuss his idea with Enrico Fermi. Fermi was just as excited about the idea of creating a chain reaction. They believed they could harness this energy to make electricity. First, though, they needed to know how much pure uranium-235 was needed to set up the chain reaction, and how they could control the potentially violent reactions.

At the same time, other scientists had realized that nuclear fission could be used in a new type of bomb: the atom bomb. In 1939, the *Physical Review* published a paper by Niels Bohr and the American John Wheeler describing their theory of nuclear fission and the importance of uranium-235. Within weeks, the Second World War began. Both Germany and the United States had information about nuclear fission. One of the scientists leading the research in Germany was Werner Heisenberg.

The world's first nuclear reactor, Chicago Pile 1, was built by Fermi and his team in the basement of a disused sports stadium in Chicago.

Enriching uranium

The main problem was getting enough of the uranium-235 to keep the chain reaction going. Uranium is found in rock. To obtain the metal, the rock has to be crushed and heated, and the metal has to be extracted and purified. Only a tiny fraction of it is uranium-235 – the rest of the uranium has no use. A huge enrichment plant was constructed at Oak Ridge, Tennessee, USA, to provide enough uranium-235 for the research.

By 1941, Fermi and his colleague Leo Szilard had drawn up the plans for a nuclear reactor. It was built the following year and called the Chicago Pile 1. The reactor consisted of rods of uranium placed within a stack of graphite (a type of carbon). In December 1942 the reactor was switched on, and within a few hours a chain reaction was under way.

Since that time, hundreds of nuclear power stations have been built in countries such as the United States, the United Kingdom, Germany, and France. In France, nuclear power supplies virtually all the country's electricity.

When an atom bomb explodes, it produces a characteristic mushroom cloud, which rises into the atmosphere.

WHAT WAS THE MANHATTAN PROJECT?

The Manhattan Project was the research carried out in the United States into using nuclear reactions to create an atom bomb. Enrico Fermi and his fellow scientists were working during the Second World War. They were interested in using nuclear power for peaceful purposes. However, governments were more interested in how the energy released from nuclear fission could be used as a weapon. Reactors based on Fermi's design were used in the Manhattan Project to produce the plutonium for atomic weapons. On 6 August 1945, the United States dropped the first atom bomb on Hiroshima in Japan.

Particle zoo

While Enrico Fermi and others were studying **nuclear fission**, other scientists were smashing atoms and discovering new subatomic particles. They discovered that the atom contained a lot more than just electrons, protons, neutrons, and their **antiparticles**. This was the era of high-energy physics.

The discovery of the subatomic particles was made possible by the invention of a machine called a particle accelerator. This works in much the same way as the cathode ray tube in a television. The cathode ray tube takes electrons from the cathode, speeds them up, and smashes them into phosphor on a screen. The high-speed collision creates a glow on the television screen.

Particle accelerators

A particle accelerator works on the same principle. However, the machines are huge, the particles are accelerated to almost the speed of light, and the collisions are more violent, to scatter the particles. The particles are accelerated by powerful **electromagnetic** fields, which push them forwards, a bit like a surfer being pushed along on the crest of a wave.

These are the tracks left by subatomic particles from a particle accelerator. When particles are passed through a chamber of liquid hydrogen they leave behind a trail of tiny bubbles. The tracks have been coloured so they can be seen more clearly.

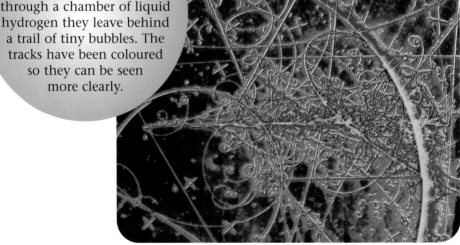

There are two types of accelerator. The first is the linear accelerator, in which the beam of particles is accelerated in a **vacuum** down a long copper tube several kilometres in length. The other is circular. In this, the beam is accelerated around the track to collide with the target. Both accelerators are built under ground. There are large detectors to record all the events that take place after the collisions.

From Cyclotron to CERN

The earliest example of a particle accelerator was the Cyclotron, which was invented by Ernest Lawrence (1901–1958) and built by his team in 1930 at Berkeley in the United States. This machine was created especially to discover the **antiproton**. It generated a beam of protons that was fired at atoms. In 1954, Lawrence built the Bevatron, which could smash two protons together to produce antiprotons. In 1955, Emilio Segre and Owen Chamberlain built a special detector for the Bevatron and became the first scientists to detect the antiproton. Soon after, another team working at the Bevatron, led by B. Cork, announced that they had found the antineutron.

THAT'S AMAZING!

Scientists at CERN have managed to produce some real **antimatter** – but only in very tiny amounts.

European scientists were also searching for subatomic particles. In 1954, the decision was made to build a huge research facility to study high-energy physics. It was called CERN (Centre for European Nuclear Research) and was built near Geneva, Switzerland. Since then, CERN has played a major role in high-energy physics.

Particles everywhere

Particle accelerators have revealed that the atom is made up of many particles. As more powerful machines were built and atoms were smashed into even smaller bits, even more particles were found. Some of these only exist for a fraction of a second, while others join up to form different particles. By 1960, there were so many different types of particles that they needed to be sorted into groups.

This is a computer image of a proton that is made up of three quarks. The quarks are held together by a strong nuclear force created by the gluons, which form a cloud around the quarks. There are two green "up" quarks and one pink "down" quark. Together they create a single positive charge.

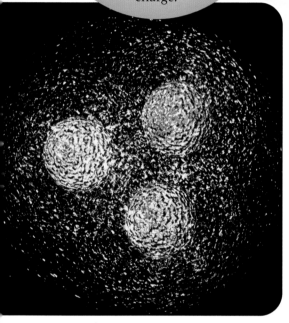

Scientists Murray Gell-Mann (b. 1929) from the United States and Yuval Ne'eman (1925–2006) from Israel came up with the same idea simultaneously. They each proposed a method for classifying all the particles. They sorted them into eight groups according to their behaviour. This method became known as the Eightfold Way. They also predicted that there were other particles still to be discovered.

Quarks and gluons

The next step was a bit surprising. In 1964, Gell-Mann and George Zweig of CERN independently proposed that protons and neutrons were not single particles. They suggested that these particles were actually made up of even smaller particles. Gell-Mann called the tiny particles **quarks**. He suggested that protons and neutrons were each made up of a cluster of three quarks held together by another particle, called a **gluon**. Each quark had a fraction of a charge: some had a partial positive charge, while others had a partial negative charge.

THAT'S AMAZING!

A sheet of aluminium foil is about 250,000 atoms thick. If you took one of those atoms and enlarged it so that it was the size of the Earth, a quark inside the **nucleus** of that atom would be no larger than your fist.

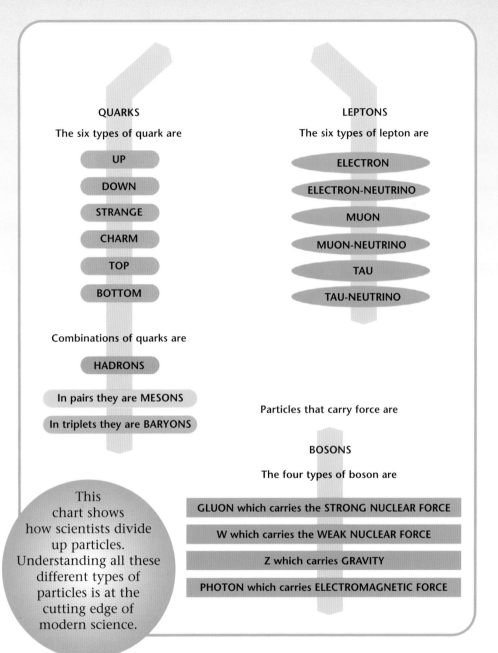

QUARKS

The six types of quark are

UP

DOWN

STRANGE

CHARM

TOP

BOTTOM

Combinations of quarks are

HADRONS

In pairs they are MESONS

In triplets they are BARYONS

LEPTONS

The six types of lepton are

ELECTRON

ELECTRON-NEUTRINO

MUON

MUON-NEUTRINO

TAU

TAU-NEUTRINO

Particles that carry force are

BOSONS

The four types of boson are

GLUON which carries the STRONG NUCLEAR FORCE

W which carries the WEAK NUCLEAR FORCE

Z which carries GRAVITY

PHOTON which carries ELECTROMAGNETIC FORCE

This chart shows how scientists divide up particles. Understanding all these different types of particles is at the cutting edge of modern science.

Proof that quarks existed came from experiments at the Stanford Linear Accelerator in the United States in 1969. All together there are six "flavours" of quarks: up, down, top, bottom, strange, and charm. Each of these six quarks has an antiquark! Quarks do not exist by themselves, only in pairs (**mesons**) or triplets (**baryons**). The bottom quark was discovered at Fermilab in the United States in 1977. The top quark was the last to be discovered, in 1995, by the scientists at Fermilab.

Frontiers of research

Scientists are learning more about the subatomic particles that make up atoms. These subatomic particles could be useful in the future – for example, for powering engines. One question often asked by scientists is "What determines **mass**?" Many of the experiments that are being carried out in particle accelerators are investigating the mechanism that causes mass.

This is the ALEPH particle detector at CERN. It is one of four giant particle detectors that are used with the Large Hadron Collider.

The largest particle accelerator in the world is the Large Hadron Collider at CERN. It consists of a narrow circular tunnel about 27 kilometres (17 miles) long. A beam of protons is whizzed around at almost the speed of light, guided by powerful magnets. Another beam of protons travels in the opposite direction. The protons smash together inside a special detector. This happens 10 million times a second. When the protons collide, they explode into smaller particles, some of which only last a fraction of a second. Smashing the protons together is the easy bit. It's much harder to interpret all the information produced every single day.

The search for the Higgs boson

The Large Hadron Collider particle accelerator cost more than US$3 billion and it was built just to find a subatomic particle called the Higgs boson. This tiny speck of **matter** is possibly the key to understanding why matter has mass. The discovery of the Higgs boson is one of the most sought-after prizes in the field of particle physics. Scientists believe that when particles interact with the Higgs boson, they gain mass.

Imagine a crowd of people awaiting the arrival of a celebrity. The celebrity arrives and creates a disturbance as he moves through the crowd. People cluster around the celebrity and he gains momentum, pushed forwards by all the people. The celebrity has gained mass. Scientists believe that this clustering effect is the Higgs mechanism.

Space travel at warp speed

In the television series *Star Trek*, the USS *Enterprise* hurtles through space at warp speeds. The warp drive engines are powered by **antimatter**. Although *Star Trek* is science fiction, the idea was based on science fact. Now engineers at NASA are designing spacecraft that are powered by antimatter. Matter–antimatter reactions are 1,000 times more powerful than **nuclear fission**. A spacecraft powered by these engines would be able to reach Mars in just one month, compared with the current nine months.

The main problem is finding antimatter. There is very little natural antimatter, so scientists have to create it. Particle accelerators such as the one at CERN make **antiprotons**, but in minuscule quantities. For example, all the antiprotons produced at CERN in a year would only be enough to light a 100-watt electric light bulb for 3 seconds. It will take about 10 grams (0.4 ounces) of antiprotons to fuel a journey to Mars.

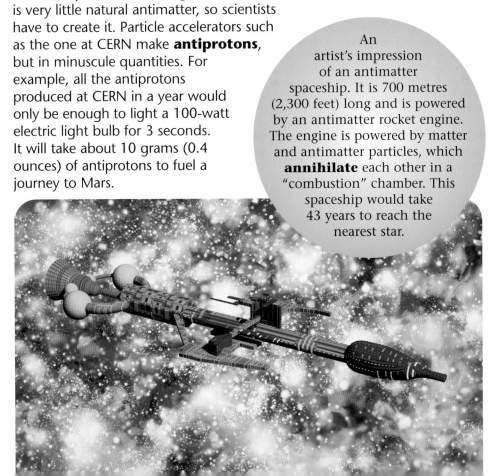

An artist's impression of an antimatter spaceship. It is 700 metres (2,300 feet) long and is powered by an antimatter rocket engine. The engine is powered by matter and antimatter particles, which **annihilate** each other in a "combustion" chamber. This spaceship would take 43 years to reach the nearest star.

Atoms today

It has taken thousands of years for scientists to work out the structure of the atom. Even now they are still discovering new things, so our understanding of atoms is improving all the time. But just as scientists think that they have worked out the structure and the role of all the different particles, another one is found. These tiny particles have been incredibly difficult to study. Not only are they far too small to be observed, but some only last for fractions of a second. It is also very expensive to study them, as particle accelerators cost billions of pounds to build and maintain.

Splitting the atom – good or bad?

Splitting the atom was a major breakthrough. However, this knowledge has been used in different ways. The energy locked up in the uranium atom can be used as a source of power to generate electricity – but at a cost. Nuclear power stations can generate large quantities of electricity from relatively small amounts of uranium fuel, but once the uranium fuel is exhausted it has to be replaced, and the uranium waste is radioactive. It has to be handled very carefully and stored for hundreds of years until it is safe.

Nuclear power is a controversial energy source. It has the potential to generate enough electricity to power the world. But it also produces hazardous waste and could be used to produce atom bombs.

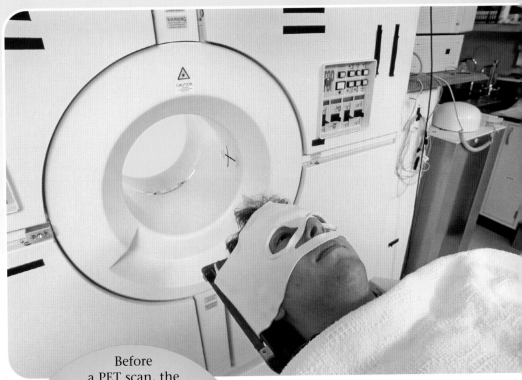

Before a PET scan, the patient is injected with a weakly radioactive liquid, which gathers in the cancer cells. This releases positrons. When a positron bumps into an electron, they annihilate each other and create high-energy radiation. The PET scanner detects this radiation. The region with the tumour will show the most activity.

There are other problems. Nuclear power can be misused. Atom bombs are powerful weapons and can cause complete devastation, as witnessed when the first two bombs were dropped on Japan in 1945. Today there are concerns that some countries might misuse nuclear technology – for example, by using nuclear power stations to generate fuel suitable for use in atom bombs.

Subatomic particles — a fuel for the future?

Much of the latest research is directed at finding subatomic particles and discovering new ways of using them. One use is in PET (**positron** emission tomography) scanners, a type of whole-body scanner that can be used to find cancerous tumours in the body. In the future it is possible that scientists will learn how to make and store antimatter. This could then be used to fuel spacecraft that will carry people to the furthest reaches of the galaxy.

Timeline

c. 400 BC Democritus proposes his theory of atoms.

c. 350 BC Aristotle proposes his theory of the four elements.

1658 Pierre Gassendi publishes *Syntagma Philosophiae Epicuri*, in which he proposes his theory of the atom.

1661 Robert Boyle publishes *The Sceptical Chymist*, in which he challenges Aristotle's theories.

1689 Edmund Halley presents his paper on gold atoms to the Royal Society.

1771–1774 Joseph Priestley carries out experiments on carbon dioxide and oxygen.

1789 Antoine Lavoisier draws up the first table of chemical elements.

1803 John Dalton publishes *New System of Chemical Philosophy*, in which he describes his atomic theory. He also publishes a table of atomic masses.

1811 Amedeo Avogadro proposes his theory that equal volumes of gases, if kept at the same temperature and pressure, would contain the same number of molecules.

1860 Stanislao Cannizzaro proves Avogadro's theory.

1869 Dmitri Mendeleev publishes his periodic table, in which the elements are organized into seven groups with similar properties.

1875 Lecoq de Boisbaudran discovers gallium, proving Mendeleev's system of organizing the elements.

1895 Wilhelm Röntgen discovers X-rays.

1897 J. J. Thomson discovers the electron.

1904 J. J. Thomson publishes his model of an atom, based on a plum pudding.

1905 Albert Einstein explains Brownian motion.

1911 Ernest Rutherford proposes his model of atomic structure.

1912 Victor Hess proves that cosmic rays come from space. Charles Wilson invents the cloud chamber.

1913 Niels Bohr suggests that electrons are found in specific levels (shells) around the nucleus

1919 Ernest Rutherford becomes the first person to split an atom and discovers the proton.

1924 Louis de Broglie suggests that electrons move in waves around the nucleus.

1928 Paul Dirac suggests that there are antiparticles.

1930 Ernest Lawrence invents the first particle accelerator.

1932 James Chadwick discovers the neutron. Carl Anderson finds antielectrons, which he calls positrons.

1934 Enrico Fermi discovers that uranium atoms can be split by bombarding them with neutrons. Hideki Yukawa explains the force between subatomic particles.

1939 Niels Bohr and John Wheeler describe the process of nuclear fission in an article in *Physical Review*.

1942 Enrico Fermi and Leo Szilard build the first nuclear reactor and create a chain reaction.

1945 The first atomic bomb is dropped on Hiroshima in Japan.

1947 Cecil Powell observes mesons in the Earth's upper atmosphere.

1960 Murray Gell-Mann and Yuval Ne'eman propose the Eightfold Way of classifying subatomic particles.

1964 Gell-Mann and George Zweig suggest that protons and neutrons are made up of quarks.

1977 The bottom quark is discovered by scientists at Fermilab in the United States.

1995 The top quark is found at Fermilab.

2005 Scientists at the Large Hadron Collider at CERN start looking for the Higgs boson.

Biographies

These are some of the leading scientists in the story of the atom.

Amedeo Avogadro (1776–1856)

Amedeo Avodagro was born and died in Turin, Italy. There were many distinguished lawyers in his family so it is not surprising that he studied law at university. However, he was more interested in the natural sciences, so in 1800 he began private studies in physics and mathematics. In 1809, he became Professor of Physics at Vercelli, where he produced his famous hypothesis on the volumes of perfect gases. His most important publication was his four-volume physics textbook, *Fisica dei corpi ponderabili*, which appeared between 1837 and 1841.

Niels Bohr (1885–1962)

Niels Henrik David Bohr was born in Copenhagen, Denmark. He studied physics at Copenhagen University. During 1911 and 1912 he visited England, where he studied with J. J. Thomson and Ernest Rutherford. He published his theory of atomic structure in 1913. In 1922 he was awarded the Nobel Prize for Physics. During the Second World War Bohr escaped to Sweden. He travelled to England and then the United States, where he became involved with the Atomic Energy Project. After the war, he devoted his work to the peaceful application of atomic physics and campaigned against the development of atomic weapons.

Robert Boyle (1627–1691)

Robert Boyle was born in Ireland and educated at the famous Eton school in England. He travelled widely in Europe. He studied science, philosophy, religion, languages, and mathematics. In 1660, he published his first major scientific paper, called *The Spring and Weight of the Air*, in which he described his experiments using a new vacuum pump. He published a second edition of this paper in 1662, which included Boyle's Law. In 1661, he published *The Sceptical Chymist*, in which he discussed his idea of elements. In 1654, he joined a group of doctors, scientists, mathematicians, and philosophers. In 1662, this group founded the Royal Society.

John Dalton (1766–1844)

John Dalton was born in Cumbria, England. He was a teacher and lecturer. He joined the Manchester Literary and Philosophical Society, which provided him with laboratory facilities so he could continue with his studies of atoms. He was also a keen meteorologist and kept daily weather records from 1787 until his death. He combined all his observations and theories into his *New System of Chemical Philosophy* (1808–1827). In his later life he received many honours and was held in great respect by the public. When he died, more than 40,000 people marched in his funeral procession through the streets of Manchester.

Murray Gell-Mann (b. 1929)

Murray Gell-Mann was born in New York in 1929. He obtained his degree at Yale University in 1948, and his doctorate in 1951 at the Massachusetts Institute of Technology. In 1952, he moved to the University of Chicago, where he worked on subatomic particles. Working with Yuval Ne'eman, he devised the Eightfold Way, which classified the 100 or so particles in the nucleus. Then he discovered that all the particles were made up of quarks. In 1969, he received the Nobel Prize for Physics. In 1994 he published a popular science book, *The Quark and the Jaguar: Adventures in the Simple and the Complex*. This explains the connections between the basic laws of physics and the complexity and diversity of the natural world.

James Clerk Maxwell (1831–1879)

The Scottish scientist James Clerk Maxwell is considered the greatest theoretical physicist of the 19th century. As well as having a great interest in science, he was also a gifted mathematician and this enabled him to make important advances in electromagnetism and the kinetic theory of gases. Maxwell provided the final proof that the movement of molecules created heat.

Dmitri Mendeleev (1834–1907)

Dmitri Mendeleev was born at Tobolsk, Siberia. He studied science at St Petersburg and became a professor in 1863. He is best known for his work on the periodic table, in which he arranged the 63 known elements into a chart based on atomic weights. He published his periodic table in the *Principles of Chemistry* in 1869. Using his table he was able to predict the existence of undiscovered elements.

Ernest Rutherford (1871–1937)

Ernest Rutherford was born in New Zealand, and came to England on a scholarship. In 1895, he began work at the Cavendish Laboratory at Cambridge University, under the guidance of J. J. Thomson. First he studied radio waves and then he looked at the newly discovered X-rays. He moved to Manchester University where, in 1911, he published his theory of atomic structure. In 1912, he and Niels Bohr refined the theory of atomic structure, which has remained virtually unchanged ever since. In 1908, Rutherford was awarded the Nobel Prize for Chemistry.

Glossary

alchemist medieval scientist who tried to turn metals into gold

annihilation when a particle and antiparticle come together and are destroyed – releasing energy

antimatter matter composed of the antiparticles of normal matter

antiparticle particle type that has exactly the same mass but the opposite charge of another particle type

antiproton antiparticle of a proton. It has the same size and mass as a proton but has a negative charge.

atmospheric pressure pressure of air on the Earth's surface

baryon subatomic particle made up of three quarks

Big Bang theory that the Universe began with a huge explosion around 13.7 billion years ago, and has been expanding since then

billiards game played on a covered table in which a cue is used to hit small, hard balls against each other

compound product of two or more elements reacting together

croquet lawn game in which the players hit wooden balls with wooden mallets (heavy sticks) through a series of arched hoops

electrode electrical conductor through which a current enters or leaves something

electromagnetism magnetism created by an electric current

element substance that cannot be broken down by chemical means (for example, oxygen and carbon)

fermenting breaking a substance down into simpler substances in the absence of oxygen

force something that holds objects together, changes an object from a state of rest to one of movement, or changes its direction or rate of motion

gluon particle that holds quarks together

gram-mole molecular weight of a substance, expressed in grams

gravity force acting between any two bodies

isotope atom of an element that has a different number of neutrons and therefore a different mass (for example, uranium U-235 and U-238)

mass measure of how much matter something contains

matter group of particles that are capable of occupying space

meson subatomic particle made up of a quark and an antiquark

microscope instrument that uses a lens to magnify objects (make them look larger)

mole basic unit amount of any substance

molecule group of atoms that are joined together in a particular way

neutrino particle with no electric charge emitted during nuclear fission

nuclear fission where the nucleus of a heavy element such as uranium splits into two parts, releasing energy as it does so

nuclear fusion where light elements such as hydrogen join together to form heavier elements – releasing energy

nucleus centre of an atom, which contains most of its mass. It has a positive charge and contains protons and neutrons.

organism any living thing – plant, animal, or bacterium – that can function independently

philosopher someone who studies philosophy – beliefs about life and religion

photon particle of light or other electromagnetic radiation, released by electrons as they lose energy

positron antiparticle of an electron. It is an equivalent particle but with positive charge.

quantum theory laws of physics that apply on very small scales. One of the key features of quantum physics is that electric charge and momentum come in amounts called quanta.

quark particle found inside protons and neutrons

radiation energy travelling in the form of electromagnetic waves

reactant substance used in a chemical reaction, usually present at the start of the reaction

supernova death of a giant star in an explosion that briefly burns as brightly as an entire galaxy

transmutation process by which each of the four "elements" – fire, earth, air, and water – can be transformed into another

vacuum region where there is no free matter, such as space

volume amount of space occupied by an object or matter

wavelength distance between one peak or trough and the next on a wave

Further resources

If you have enjoyed this book and want to find out more, you can look at the following books and websites.

Books

Atoms
Don Nardo
(Kidhaven Press, 2001)

Atoms
Chris Oxlade
(Heinemann Library, 2002)

Atoms and Elements
David Bradley and Ian Crofton
(Oxford University Press, 2002)

Hiroshima, The Story of the First Atom Bomb
Clive A. Lawton
(Franklin Watts, 2004)

Nuclear Energy
Nigel Saunders and Steven Chapman
(Raintree, 2005)

Nuclear Energy
Robert Sneddon
(Heinemann Library, 2006)

Splitting the Atom
Alan Morton
(Evans Books, 2005)

A Weird History of Science: Foolish Physics
John Townsend
(Raintree, 2006)

Websites

Jefferson Laboratory
http://education.jlab.org/index.html
Lots of information in the student section on atoms, including some useful Q and A sections.

CERN
http://public.web.cern.ch/public/
The world's largest particle physics laboratory has information about the latest developments.

Antimatter: Mirror of the Universe
http://livefromcern.web.cern.ch/livefromcern/antimatter/index.html
Website produced by CERN about antimatter: what it is, its history, and how it can be used.

You can also search for more information by putting key words into a search engine. Here are some suggestions:

Alchemists
Atom bomb
Manhattan Project
Nuclear fission
Periodic table
Robert Boyle

Index

Titles in the *Chain Reactions* series include:

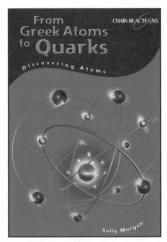

Hardback 978 0 431 18657 3

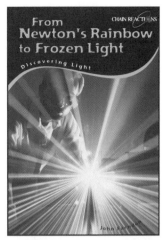

Hardback 978 0 431 18658 0

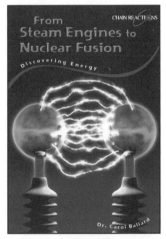

Hardback 978 0 431 18659 7

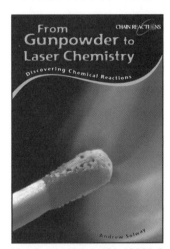

Hardback 978 0 431 18660 3

Hardback 978 0 431 18661 0

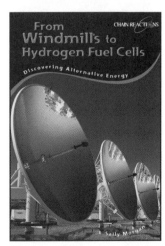

Hardback 978 0 431 18662 7

Find out about other titles from Heinemann Library on our website www.heinemann.co.uk/library